GROSS DARKNESS
-WINNING THE BATTLE AGAINST DEPRESSION-

Joyce Oyelade

TABLE OF CONTENTS:

Copyright Page

Gross Darkness - Winning the Battle Against Depression
© 2023 Copyright Joyce Oyelade
ISBN 9798862128086

For more information, email chikel1104@gmail.com

Introduction

This book is dedicated to helping individuals overcome the challenges of depression and emerge victorious. It is a comprehensive guide that offers practical tips, strategies, and techniques to combat the debilitating effects of depression. Joyce Oyelade has spent years researching and studying the topic and has developed a wealth of knowledge and insights that are shared within the pages of this book.

The book begins by providing a detailed explanation of what depression is, its causes, symptoms, and the way in which it affects individuals. It then goes on to explore the different types of depression, such as major depressive disorder, bipolar disorder, and seasonal affective disorder, among several others. Overall, this book is a valuable resource for anyone struggling with depression or knows someone who is. It provides a comprehensive guide to understanding and treating depression and offers practical tips and strategies for managing symptoms and improving one's overall well-being. One of the unique aspects of this book is its emphasis on the spiritual aspect of depression.

The author recognizes that depression can have a profound impact on an individual's faith and provides guidance on how to navigate this aspect of depression. She also addresses the common misconceptions surrounding depression treatment, such as the belief that medication is the only effective treatment option. Oyelade has a deep understanding of the struggles that people face when dealing with depression. This book is a valuable resource for those who are seeking to overcome depression and regain control of their lives.

The book also includes a section on how to cope with depression, providing practical tips and strategies for managing symptoms and improving one's overall well-being. *Gross Darkness- Winning the Battle Against Depression* concludes with a message of hope and encouragement, reminding readers that recovery is possible, and that they can overcome depression and live a fulfilling life.

Understanding Depression

Depression is a prevalent mental illness that affects a significant portion of the global population. In the United States alone, over 16 million adults are impacted by depression each year, while the worldwide number reaches a staggering 264 million. What makes depression particularly daunting is that it can strike anyone at any point in their life, regardless of age or background. Unfortunately, even Christians are not exempt from experiencing depression, and it can be especially difficult for them to manage. This is partly due to the stigma associated with depression and with many Christians viewing it as a sign of weakness.

Depression is a sensitive topic that is often avoided in conversations. It is not simply a passing feeling of sadness that most experience occasionally. It is a deep sense of hopelessness that makes even the things that were once enjoyable seem meaningless; a constant battle for those who suffer from it. Chronic, or long-term, depression can leave individuals feeling overwhelmingly sad for extended periods, with a loss of enjoyment for their daily activities. This condition results from unexpected negative changes in life. Depression affects people's emotions, thoughts, and behaviors, leading to physical and emotional issues.

According to the bible, we are called to comfort those who are mourning in Zion by giving them roses instead of ashes, joyful messages instead of news of doom, and a heart full of praise instead of a spirit that is weak. This passage from Isaiah 61:3 teaches us that we are like "Oaks of Righteousness" planted by God to display his glory. The bible also tells us that depression is a spirit that can cause a feeling of heaviness and oppression, which could steal our faith and bring us down. Therefore, we must be vigilant in caring for those who are struggling with depression and help them find ways to overcome it.

It has been determined that a significant portion of the adult population in the United States, approximately 6.7%, experience the effects of depression. This condition is particularly prevalent in individuals aged between 18 and 25 years, with an occurrence rate of 10.9%, and those who belong to more than one racial group, with a rate of 10.5%. Women are twice as likely as men to experience an episode of depression, as noted both by the National Institute of Mental Health (NIMH) and the World Health Organization (WHO).

Recent data from the Centers for Disease Control and Prevention (CDC) reveals that between 2013 and 2016, 10.4% of women were diagnosed with depression, compared to just 5.5% of men. The WHO has estimated that over 300 million people worldwide are affected by depression.

Chapter 1
The Hidden Truth About Depression

Chapter 1
The Hidden Truth About Depression

Depression is more than just a state of mind; it is a battle that extends to the spiritual realm. It is not simply a matter of experiencing negative thoughts or difficult emotions, but rather a culmination of various factors, such as past traumas, current struggles, and the accumulation of negativity. Even individuals who have access to significant financial resources can find themselves grappling with depression, proving that it is not affected by economic factors. Contrary to the popular belief that depression stems solely from imbalances in brain chemistry, its roots extend far beyond the physical realm.

By acknowledging the spiritual dimension of depression, we can approach its treatment and healing with a more holistic perspective. It is important to recognize that depression, anxiety, and other mental health challenges are not purely psychological in nature; they possess a spiritual component as well. Having worked in the healthcare field for three decades, I have witnessed firsthand the intimate connection between a person's spiritual and psychological well-being.

These issues can manifest in various forms, such as post-traumatic stress syndrome, panic attacks, and even thoughts of suicide. Addressing the spiritual aspect of mental health is crucial to attaining genuine peace and joy in one's life. When depression takes hold, it feels like a heavy cloud that lingers, persisting even in the face of prayer and fasting. It is not solely a psychological issue, but rather a spiritual one caused by a malevolent force known as the Spirit of Heaviness. This spirit has a distinct personality, targeting an individual's vulnerabilities and launching attacks at an opportune moment.

Moreover, the Bible not only enlightens us about the nature of these battles but also cautions us about the tactics employed by our spiritual adversary. It warns us of the enemy's cunning strategies, which involve infiltrating our minds with false thoughts and deceitful lies. These insidious tactics can lead to detrimental consequences, such as depression and other mental struggles.

Therefore, it becomes imperative for us to be fully aware of the spiritual battles that surround us, constantly seeking to equip ourselves with the necessary tools and weapons to counteract them effectively. In essence, the Bible urges us to be ever vigilant and discerning; to recognize that our struggles extend beyond the physical realm. It emphasizes the need for us to fortify ourselves with the all-encompassing armor of God, enabling us to stand firm in our beliefs and convictions, even amidst the most challenging and evil circumstances.

By acknowledging the existence of these spiritual battles and actively engaging in the fight against them, we can emerge victorious and experience the profound transformation that comes from aligning ourselves with the divine power and protection. The Bible serves as a constant reminder that the battles we face in our lives are not merely physical in nature but rather they are spiritual in essence. It emphasizes the importance of engaging in a continuous struggle against the rulers, authorities, and powers of darkness, along with the spiritual forces of evil that exist in the heavenly realms.

To confront and overcome these spiritual battles effectively, we are called upon to prepare ourselves by putting on the full armor of God and remaining unwavering in our faith, even when confronted with the presence of evil. This powerful message, contained in Ephesians 6:12-13, serves as a guiding principle for believers to always be ready and equipped to combat the forces of darkness.

Chapter 2

Understanding the Causes and Types of Depression

WINNING THE BATTLE AGAINST DEPRESSION.

Chapter 2
Understanding the Causes and Types of Depression

Depression is a common issue that affects people from different walks of life, including Christians. While it can be caused by spiritual factors, such as a loss of faith or a feeling of disconnection from God, it can also be triggered by physical factors, such as hormonal imbalances or genetic predisposition. In fact, studies have shown that depression is often linked to a chemical imbalance in the brain, which affects a person's mood and emotional state. Despite the complex nature of depression, the Bible offers a simple yet powerful message of hope. Proverbs 12:25 reminds us that anxiety and worry can lead to depression, but a kind and positive word can lift our spirits and bring joy to our hearts. This verse highlights the importance of empathy, compassion, and encouragement in supporting those who are struggling with depression.

Many individuals who struggle with depression report feeling lost, directionless, and unsure of their purpose in life. This lack of purpose can lead to feelings of despair, hopelessness, and a sense of meaninglessness. Without a sense of purpose, individuals may feel that their lives lack significance, which can exacerbate symptoms of depression and anxiety. One of the primary spiritual causes of depression is a disconnection from one's true self. Living in a society that values material wealth, success, and external validation over inner growth and authenticity can lead to a sense of emptiness and disconnection. When individuals feel disconnected from their inner selves, they may experience feelings of loneliness, isolation, and a general sense of dissatisfaction with life.

This sense of disconnection can lead to a lack of motivation, apathy, and a sense of hopelessness, which are all common symptoms of depression. Exploring the spiritual causes of depression can be an essential step in addressing this mental health condition. By connecting with one's inner self, finding purpose and meaning in life, and cultivating a sense of connection with a higher power or spiritual energy, individuals can begin to heal and move towards a more fulfilling and joyful life.

By examining the factors that lead to depression through a spiritual lens, we can uncover further underlying causes for it. There are various factors that can contribute to these causes, many of which can be traced back to unresolved emotional pain. One such example is the experience of heartbreak or the aftermath of a broken relationship. To illustrate this, consider the case of a lady who was deeply devastated when her fiancé abruptly ended their engagement and chose to be with another woman. The intense emotional turmoil she endured because of this betrayal led her down a dark path, plunging her into a state of profound depression that nearly drove her to the brink of taking her own life.

Experiencing a sense of aimlessness or uncertainty, along with feelings of being alone or detached from others and from one's own spirituality, can contribute to the development of depression. In certain instances, depression may arise as a manifestation of a spiritual crisis, wherein an individual feels a profound sense of being adrift and disconnected from their inherent purpose in life.

Depression can emerge from a multitude of factors, with one such cause being the experience of death or a loss. As a personal testament, I found myself spiraling into a deep state of depression when I tragically lost my beloved father. Throughout this harrowing journey, I encountered and traversed through all the stages of grief and mourning, grappling with immense sorrow and despair. The weight of my father's death was so profound that it manifested itself physically. My appetite dwindled and my body struggled to adapt to the painful reality that I would never have the privilege of seeing my father's face or hearing his voice again.

Depression may also arise from various forms of abuse, including physical, emotional, verbal, or a combination of the three. The detrimental effects of abuse can manifest in the form of diminished self-esteem and overwhelming feelings of shame. Consequently, individuals who have experienced abuse during their formative years may be more prone to engaging in further abusive relationships during their adult lives.

Major events and important milestones in life have the capacity to evoke feelings of sadness and melancholy. Events such as weddings, graduation ceremonies, and the birth of a child. These significant occurrences often bring about a mix of emotions, ranging from joy and excitement to a sense of loss or longing. While these events are typically seen as joyous occasions, they can also serve as reminders of the passage of time and the changes that come with it. This can lead individuals to reflect on their own lives and potentially experience sadness or depression.

When individuals have personal issues, such as financial debt, they can potentially trigger the onset of depression. This is due to the overwhelming stress and anxiety that comes with the burden of debt. This stress can lead to a sense of hopelessness and the feeling of being trapped in a dire situation. Such negative emotions can have a significant impact on an individual's mental health, leading to a decline in their overall well-being. Therefore, it is important to address and find solutions to personal problems in order to prevent the onset or exacerbation of depression.

It is possible for individuals to experience depression because of natural disasters. Such events can have a profound impact on mental health, causing feelings of sadness, hopelessness, and despair. The devastation and destruction wrought by these disasters can result in the loss of homes, possessions, and even loved ones. This can lead to grief that can be difficult to overcome. The trauma of experiencing a natural disaster can also cause long-term psychological effects, known as post-traumatic stress disorder (PTSD).

It is important for individuals who have been affected by natural disasters to seek emotional support and professional help to manage their mental health. Worry can also contribute to the development of depression. It is a well-established fact that excessive worrying, overthinking, and dwelling on negative thoughts can have detrimental effects on one's mental health, potentially leading to the onset of depression. When individuals constantly ruminate on their problems and fears, it can create a vicious cycle of negative emotions and thoughts, ultimately leading to a state of depression.

The constant strain and burden of worry can overwhelm individuals, causing them to lose motivation, interest, and pleasure in their daily activities. Moreover, worry can disrupt sleep patterns, appetite, and overall well-being, exacerbating the risk of depression. It is crucial to recognize the significant impact that worry might have on mental health and to take proactive steps to manage and alleviate these concerns in order to prevent the potential development of depression.

Constantly involving yourself in the matters of other people can potentially result in the development of depression. Proverbs 26:17 states that "Interfering in someone else's argument is as foolish as yanking a dog's ears." Disregarding personal boundaries and the boundaries of other people can have detrimental effects on one's mental well-being, leading to a state of prolonged sadness, hopelessness, and despair.

Interfering in the business of others can contribute to feelings of inadequacy, as it often involves comparing oneself to another person and feeling the pressure to measure up to their perceived success or happiness. This constant preoccupation with external factors can prevent individuals from focusing on their own goals, aspirations, and self-improvement, ultimately hindering their personal growth and contentment. Moreover, not respecting the privacy and boundaries of other people can strain relationships and lead to conflicts, further exacerbating feelings of isolation. In addition, constant involvement in others' affairs can result in exhaustion and burnout as it requires a significant amount of energy and emotional investment.

This depletion of resources can make individuals more susceptible to the negative effects of stress and can contribute to the development of depressive symptoms. Therefore, it is crucial to prioritize self-care, establish healthy boundaries, and respect the autonomy and privacy of others to maintain optimal mental well-being and prevent the onset of depression.

Suffering from pain, injury, or illness can lead to feelings of depression. The physical discomfort and limitations that come with these conditions can create a sense of hopelessness and sadness, as well as a loss of enjoyment in activities that were once pleasurable. Additionally, the stress and anxiety that often accompany these conditions can further contribute to the development of depression. It is important for individuals who are experiencing pain, injury, or illness to seek support from healthcare professionals and loved ones to help manage both their physical and emotional well-being. Without proper care and attention, the negative impact of these conditions on mental health can persist and worsen over time.

Depression is often a factor that adds complexity to chronic illnesses. This means that people who suffer from chronic illnesses are more likely to experience depression, which can further impact their overall health and quality of life. Battling with depression can make it harder to manage chronic illness symptoms, as it can sap motivation and energy, and make it more difficult to engage in self-care and other healthy behaviors. Additionally, depression can exacerbate physical symptoms of chronic illness, such as pain, fatigue, and sleep disturbances. It is important for healthcare providers to be aware of the high prevalence of depression in patients with chronic illnesses, and to provide appropriate treatment and support. By addressing both physical and mental health concerns, patients can improve their overall well-being and better manage their chronic illnesses.

Conflict in families can impact children's mental and emotional well-being, leading to stress, anxiety, and depression. As 2 Timothy 2:23 advises, it's important to avoid unproductive and argumentative conversations that can cause more harm than good.

There are some medications that have been identified as having the potential to increase the likelihood of developing depression. As a result, the use of these medications may be associated with an increased risk of developing depression. It is important to be aware of these potential side effects and to speak with a healthcare professional if any symptoms of depression occur while taking medication.

By being proactive and seeking the necessary treatment, individuals can minimize the risk of developing depression and improve their overall health and well-being.

Sinful behavior can cause individuals to feel disconnected from God, others and their own moral compass, leading to loneliness and depression. Keeping secrets and facing the consequences of sinful behavior can also contribute to depression. Sin can damage relationships and cause legal issues, causing external stressors that make it harder to cope with internal struggles. Sin can have a profound impact on mental health, causing feelings of guilt, shame, worthlessness, negative self-talk, and self-blame. This can lead to a sense of hopelessness and despair. Seeking help is important to break free from negative emotions and behaviors.

Types of Depression
Major Depressive Disorder is the most common type of depression, with symptoms including insomnia, feelings of hopelessness and guilt, loss of interest in activities, and persistent sadness. Situational depression is a short-term type of depression caused by a stressful event or series of events, such as relationship problems or the death of a loved one. Symptoms include sadness, difficulty carrying out daily activities, and disinterest in food.

Peripartum depression, also known as postpartum depression, is a type of depression that affects some women after childbirth. It is different from what is known as the baby blues and can last longer, causing intense symptoms, such as feelings of worthlessness and difficulty bonding with the baby. About 10-15% of women experience postpartum depression. Seasonal affective disorder is another type of depression that occurs during specific seasons, particularly in the fall and winter. Symptoms include social withdrawal, low energy, overeating, and weight gain. These symptoms are believed to be caused by a lack of exposure to sunlight.

Summer seasonal affective disorder has symptoms such as loss of appetite, leading to weight loss, difficulty sleeping, feeling agitated, restless, and anxious, as well as having episodes of violent behavior.

Post-Traumatic Stress Disorder (PTSD) is a mental disorder caused by experiencing or witnessing traumatic events such as accidents, a war or sexual assault. PTSD can cause nightmares, anxiety, and panic triggered by the memory of the event.

Substance-induced Mood Disorder (SIMD) is caused by substance abuse and can trigger changes in mood, thinking, and behavior that can last for days or weeks. Symptoms include low energy levels, sadness, physical symptoms, trouble sleeping, changes in appetite and weight, loss of interest, hopelessness, and suicidal thoughts. Substance abuse can worsen depression even if it provides temporary relief. Almost 30% of people with substance abuse problems also have major depression.

Psychotic depression is a type of major depression where the person experiences severe depression as well as psychotic symptoms such as hallucinations, false beliefs, and paranoia. Other symptoms include agitation, anxiety, insomnia, and physical immobility.

Chapter 3

Depression in the Life of a Christian

Chapter 3
Depression in the Life of a Christian

Christian Depression is a battle that takes place in the spiritual realm. This type of depression is typically marked by a diminished sense of spiritual energy and happiness. Specifically, within the context of Christianity, undergoing a spiritual depression may entail losing connection with one's faith, neglecting the presence of God, or encountering difficulty in allocating time for spiritual growth. Additionally, it may involve becoming consumed by dwelling on past errors instead of embracing the potential for personal growth and improvement. Overall, a prevailing feeling of discontentment or sadness may pervade one's spiritual state during such periods of depression.

Many individuals who are going through a period of spiritual depression frequently express a sense of disconnection or separation from their spiritual beliefs or a feeling of being distanced from God. This disconnection may result in feelings of isolation and detachment from their faith or spiritual beliefs.

There may be times when you experience uncertainty or disappointment in your religious beliefs, struggling to communicate with God or feeling as though your prayers go unanswered. This can lead to confusion, frustration, and a sense of distance from the divine. It's important to recognize that these feelings are normal, and that there are steps you can take to strengthen your faith and reconnect with your spirituality. Don't be afraid to seek guidance from trusted religious leaders or to explore different approaches to worship and prayer. Remember that faith is a journey, and it's okay to have moments of doubt or difficulty along the way. With patience, perseverance, and a willingness to seek support and guidance, you can overcome these challenges and deepen your relationship with God.

In addition to the aforementioned indicators, there are several other important signals to look out for.

If you're having trouble finding happiness in your religious practices, are distancing yourself from your church or religious community, avoiding interaction with other members, losing interest in regular activities, or performing them out of obligation, it's possible that you're experiencing a lack of meaning in your religious pursuits. If you find that you're no longer comforted by prayer and are beginning to think negatively about your faith or God, you may be questioning or doubting your beliefs.

These feelings can lead to a sense of hopelessness or discouragement, which can also impact your personal relationships. You may feel unable to share your struggles with your partner or feel that they don't understand what you're going through. This can add to your frustration and distress. In the book of Colossians, we find a prayer that can be helpful in addressing these issues. Verse 9 states that we should pray to be filled with the knowledge of God's will and spiritual understanding. This prayer can be adapted for our own needs and circumstances, asking for insight into our lives as God's children and the wisdom to understand our situation considering the finished work of Jesus on the cross. By understanding the truth of God's word, we can find hope and deliverance from oppression. The words of Jesus promise abundant life, freedom from captivity, and victory through the power of the Blood of the Lamb.

However, we must accept these words as true and persevere in faith to overcome oppression. Losing hope can be a major obstacle in this process, but by relying on the truth of scripture and trusting in Jesus, our hope can be restored, and we can find freedom.

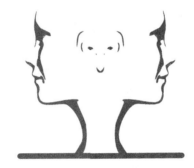

Chapter 4

The Biblical "Faces" of Depression

Chapter 4
The Biblical "Faces" of Depression

In the Bible, we can find instances of various biblical figures who exhibited classic signs of depression. These examples serve as a reminder that even those who are considered faithful and righteous can struggle with mental health issues. Many people feel that struggling with depression indicates a lack of faith and may even be considered sinful. However, numerous individuals in the Bible also experienced depression and emerged victorious. By exploring their stories, we can gain insight into how to overcome our own struggles and realize that we possess the strength to do so. It is important to remember that depression does not define our worth as believers and that we can find hope and healing through God's grace.

Elijah: (1 Kings 19: 1-5)
In 1 Kings 19:4, Elijah can be heard saying, "I have had enough, Lord. Take my life; I am no better than my ancestors." These words demonstrate the depths of his despair and the sense of hopelessness that he felt. Despite his previous victories and successes, Elijah had reached a point where he felt that he could no longer continue. Elijah, one of the strongest and most faithful followers of the Lord, found himself in a state of despair. Despite his numerous triumphs and successes, he was suddenly overcome with feelings of discouragement, weariness, rejection, and fear. These emotions were so intense that he even began to contemplate taking his own life. This story serves as a reminder that even the most faithful and devoted believers can experience moments of doubt, fear, and despair. It is important to remember that these emotions are a normal part of the human experience and that we can always turn to God for comfort and support. With faith and perseverance, we can overcome even the most challenging circumstances and emerge stronger and more resilient than ever before. This incredible turnaround in Elijah's state of mind came after a confrontation with a woman named Jezebel, who had threatened his life. Despite his unwavering faith in the Lord, Elijah was terrified and fled to save his life. It was at this point that he cried out to God, expressing his despair and hopelessness.

It's important to note that Elijah's struggles are relatable to many people today. Even the most faithful and strong believers can experience times of doubt, fear, and despair. However, Elijah's story also teaches us that we can turn to God in these moments and find strength and hope in His presence.

David: (Psalms 38:4, Psalms 42:11, 2 Samuel 12:15-23, and 2 Samuel 12:18-33)

David's trust in those around him was often betrayed, causing him great pain and disappointment. As a result, he lived a life of constant hiding, avoiding his enemies who sought to take his life. Throughout his life, David wrote numerous psalms that revealed his deep-seated feelings of loneliness, fear, and anguish, as well as his heartfelt cries for forgiveness for his sins. Additionally, David was also no stranger to the pain of losing his own children, which added to his already heavy burden of grief. David was a valiant warrior who was highly regarded by God, who saw him as a man with a heart like his own. Despite this, David was often overcome with immense feelings of sadness and despair, and his heart was filled with a sense of desolation. He spent many nights crying uncontrollably, unable to shake off the heavy burden of his emotions.

Job: (Job 2:9, Job 3:11, Job 3:26, Job 30:15-17)

Job was a man who was dedicated to serving God, living his life righteously and justly. However, despite his unwavering faith, he was met with tremendous adversity that caused him to suffer immense losses, both physical and emotional. When he lost all he had, Job's physical condition deteriorated to the point where he was in great pain and distress. Even his own wife, who also suffered from the same tragedy, urged him to curse God and end his life. Despite his commitment to God, Job struggled with his pain and despair, at one point even cursing the day he was born. He felt no peace, no calmness, and no relief. Only constant turmoil and torment. His suffering was so profound that it seemed unbearable, yet he never lost his faith in God.

Jonah: (Jonah 4:3, Jonah 4:9)

When God summoned Jonah to travel to Nineveh and spread His message to the people, Jonah attempted to escape as far away from his duty as possible. However, because of his disobedience, he experienced a tumultuous storm at sea, was swallowed by a colossal fish, and was ultimately rescued and granted another opportunity to fulfill his task. Eventually, Jonah complied and conveyed God's message to the inhabitants of Nineveh, which emphasized the availability of God's mercy to anyone who sought Him. Despite God's benevolence and upon witnessing the people of Nineveh turning away from their wicked ways and seeking redemption, Jonah reacted with resentment instead of gratitude and satisfaction.

In his despair, Jonah cried out to the Lord, pleading for his life to be taken away. He believed that death would be a more desirable alternative to living in his current state of misery. His plea reflected his overwhelming sense of hopelessness and desperation, as he had previously attempted to flee from God's calling and was now facing the consequences of his disobedience.
Despite his despair, Jonah's cry was also a testament to his faith in God's power and sovereignty, as he recognized that only the Lord had the power to grant him relief from his suffering. Ultimately, Jonah's plea for death served as a powerful reminder of the importance of obedience and the consequences that come with going against God's will.

Despite God showing great compassion towards Jonah and reaching out to him again, Jonah still expressed his anger and frustration by saying that he was so upset that he would rather die. This response from Jonah shows that he was still struggling to accept God's plan and was holding onto his own emotions and desires instead of trusting in God's wisdom and guidance. Despite his initial disobedience and stubbornness, God continued to show mercy towards Jonah and patiently worked with him to help him understand the importance of following His will.

Moses:

Depression is a complex and multifaceted mental health condition that can affect anyone, regardless of their status or achievements. Moses' story serves as a poignant reminder that even those who appear strong and successful can be plagued by inner turmoil and emotional pain. The burden of leadership often took its toll on Moses, leaving him feeling overwhelmed and isolated. Despite his close relationship with God and the support of his brother Aaron, Moses found it difficult to escape the grip depression had on him. The weight of his responsibilities seemed insurmountable at times, leading him to question his own abilities and worth.

Throughout his life, Moses faced numerous challenges and hardships, which undoubtedly contributed to his depressive episodes. From his early days of leading the Israelites out of Egypt to his long and arduous journey through the wilderness, Moses bore the weight of immense responsibility and the constant pressure of leading a nation. The story of Moses and his battle with depression is one that sheds light on the struggles many individuals face with their mental health. Moses, a prominent figure in religious history, experienced periods of deep sadness despite his significant role as a leader and prophet. Moses' battle with depression also reveals the importance of seeking help and support. Despite his unique relationship with God, Moses recognized the need to rely on others during his darkest moments. In the book of Numbers, Moses' struggle becomes evident when he pleads with God to take his life. This desperate cry for relief highlights the depths of his despair and the intensity of his inner pain. It serves as a powerful reminder that depression can rob individuals of hope and the will to live, regardless of their spiritual beliefs or strong support systems.

The story of Moses and his struggle with depression ultimately offers a message of hope and resilience. Despite his mental health struggles, Moses continued to fulfill his role as a prophet, eventually leading the Israelites to the Promised Land. His story serves as a reminder that even amid darkness, there is always the possibility for redemption and renewal.

Chapter 5

Depression | Coping with Suicidal Thoughts

Chapter 5
Depression | Coping with Suicidal Thoughts

Depression and life crises have the potential to instill within us a deep sense of hopelessness, leading us to believe that our existence lacks any meaning or value. However, it is crucial for us to recognize that this perception is far from reality. In fact, every single individual inhabiting this planet holds an innate worth and significance that surpasses the personal struggles they may be enduring. This truth becomes even more profound when we consider the sacrifice made by Jesus Christ, who, as mentioned in Romans 5:8, willingly gave up his life in order to redeem and save each and every person. This powerful act of love demonstrates that, regardless of our circumstances or emotional state, we are cherished and esteemed beyond measure. Thus, it is imperative that we firmly grasp this truth and remind ourselves that our lives possess immeasurable worth, even during the darkest moments.

In some cases, depression can become so overwhelming that individuals may start to entertain suicidal thoughts as a means of escaping their pain.

The incessant need to conform and be accepted can be particularly detrimental to one's mental well-being. Fear of judgment and rejection from peers can create an environment where individuals feel they must constantly mold themselves into a particular image or persona, forsaking their own true selves in the process. This incessant quest for validation can be mentally exhausting, leaving people emotionally drained and vulnerable to depressive episodes. One of the significant reasons for individuals succumbing to depression and ultimately contemplating suicide is the constant pressure to compete and conform to societal expectations. In today's hyper-connected world, people often find themselves tirelessly striving to emulate others, desperately attempting to measure up to certain standards set by society. The perpetual worry about how one is perceived by others can become an overwhelming burden, leading to feelings of inadequacy, hopelessness, and a sense of isolation. Moreover, the pervasive influence of social media exacerbates these feelings of inadequacy. With platforms that showcase carefully curated highlight reels, individuals often find themselves comparing their own realities to the seemingly perfect lives of others.

The constant bombardment of seemingly unattainable standards can be overwhelmingly demoralizing, leading individuals to believe that they are inferior or unworthy. This distorted perception of reality can significantly contribute to a downward spiral of self-doubt, anxiety, and ultimately, suicidal thoughts. Suicide is an immense tragedy that affects not only the individual whose life is tragically lost but also the surviving family members and friends who are left behind to grapple with their own sense of grief, emptiness, guilt, failure, and shame. Unfortunately, the global rate of suicide is alarming, and it is crucial to understand some of the underlying factors that contribute to it. In addition to external pressures, internal struggles also play a large role in the contemplation of suicide. Constant self-criticism, self-doubt, and negative self-talk can gradually erode one's self-esteem and self-worth. The perceived inability to live up to one's own expectations, or the expectations placed upon them by others, can create a profound sense of failure and shame. These feelings can be further exacerbated in a society that often stigmatizes mental health issues, making it even more challenging for individuals to seek help or confide in others about their struggles.

When faced with suicidal thoughts, individuals may seek solace in various coping mechanisms. One potential avenue for finding solace and strength is through biblical teachings and principles. The Bible offers a multitude of verses and stories that can help people navigate the crushing darkness of depression and find hope in times of anguish. One important aspect of coping with suicidal thoughts from a biblical perspective is turning to God in prayer. The act of prayer allows one to express their deepest emotions and fears to the divine, seeking comfort and guidance. By surrendering their pain and burdens to God, individuals can find solace in knowing that they are not alone in their struggles and that there is a greater power at work. Additionally, biblical teachings emphasize the importance of community and seeking support from fellow believers. Sharing one's struggles with trusted friends, family, or even a pastor can provide a sense of connection and understanding. In the book of Ecclesiastes, it is written, "Two are better than one, because they have a good return for their labor. If either of them falls down, one can help the other up. But pity anyone who falls and has no one to help them up." (Ecclesiastes 4:9-10, NIV).

This encourages individuals to lean on others during times of darkness and to seek out companionship and support. Furthermore, the Bible emphasizes the power of hope and the belief in a brighter future. In Romans 15:13 (NIV) it states, "May the God of hope fill you with all joy and peace as you trust in him, so that you may overflow with hope by the power of the Holy Spirit." This verse reminds individuals that their current circumstances do not define their future and that there is always a possibility for healing and restoration.

Furthermore, practicing gratitude and focusing on the positive aspects of life can be a biblical way of coping with suicidal thoughts. The Bible encourages individuals to give thanks in all circumstances and to focus on the good things that God has provided. By intentionally cultivating a grateful mindset, individuals can shift their focus away from despair and towards gratitude, which can help alleviate suicidal thoughts and foster a more hopeful outlook. One biblical method of coping with suicidal thoughts is through prayer and seeking a deeper connection with God. In moments of anguish, individuals can turn to prayer as a means of expressing their struggles and seeking comfort. By opening up to God and sharing their burdens, people may find a sense of relief and understanding. Additionally, seeking a deeper connection with God through regular prayer can provide a source of hope and strength during difficult times.

Chapter 6

Dealing with Depression (Biblical Solutions for Depression)

Chapter 6
Dealing with Depression (Biblical Solutions for Depression)

Depression is like a big cloud that covers up our happiness and makes life sad and dark. Sometimes we can feel good one day and the next day we wake up feeling upset for no reason. But if we change some things in our lives, and alter our perspective, we can make the cloud go away and turn the day around.

How Do We Deal with Depression?

BE FILLED WITH JOY:
"Rejoice in the Lord always. I will say it again: Rejoice!" (Philippians 4:4).
One way to avoid depression is by cultivating a sense of happiness and contentment. Filling oneself with joy and positivity can help ward off negative thoughts and emotions that often lead to depression. By focusing on the good things in life, one can create a mental state that is less susceptible to the harmful effects of stress and anxiety. This can be achieved through various activities, such as spending time with loved ones, engaging in hobbies and interests, practicing mindfulness and gratitude, and seeking professional help when needed. By prioritizing joy and happiness, one can improve their mental well-being and avoid the pitfalls of depression.

BE RESPONSIVE TO PEOPLE:
"Let your gentleness be evident to all." (Philippians 4:5)
It is important to be attentive and receptive to others when you are experiencing feelings of depression. It is crucial to recognize the impact that depression can have on your social interactions and to make a conscious effort to stay engaged with those around you. Being responsive and actively participating in social situations can help combat the isolating effects of depression and foster a sense of connection and support. It may be challenging to summon the energy and motivation to engage with others, but prioritizing social interactions can ultimately improve your mood and provide a source of comfort during difficult times.

In a world that can often be harsh and unforgiving, it can be challenging to maintain a gentle spirit. However, by focusing on the example of Christ and relying on the strength and guidance of God, we can strive to be gentle and compassionate towards all those we encounter. Through our actions, we can demonstrate the love and grace of God, and be a beacon in a dark world. So let us make every effort to make our gentleness be evident to all, knowing that the Lord is near us and supporting us every step of the way. In the book of Philippians, chapter four verse five, it is written that we should display our gentleness for all to see. We must be kind, patient, and considerate towards others, showing compassion and empathy in all our interactions. This is an important aspect of our character and, as followers of Jesus Christ, it is something that should be evident in our daily lives and interactions with others. Furthermore, the verse reminds us that the Lord is nearby. This means that we are not alone in our efforts to display gentleness and kindness towards others. We have the support and guidance of God, who is always with us and ready to help us live out our faith in practical ways. This knowledge should give us confidence and motivation to continue striving towards a gentle and loving disposition.

BE PRAYERFUL:
"Do not be anxious about anything, but in everything, by prayer and petition, with thanksgiving, present your requests to God. And the peace of God, which transcends all understanding, will guard your hearts and your minds in Christ Jesus." (Philippians 4:6-7).

Ultimately, prayer is not just about asking for things or receiving answers to our problems. It is about building a relationship with God and drawing ourselves closer to Him. Through prayer, we can find comfort, guidance, and strength to face the challenges of life and to live in a way that honors God and blesses others. When we pray, we should do so with confidence and trust that God will hear our prayers and answer them according to His will. Even if we don't always receive the answers we want, we can rest assured that God has a plan for our lives and that all things work together for our good. Prayer can take many forms and can be done in a variety of ways.

Whether we are offering up a quick prayer of thanks or spending hours in deep meditation, the act of prayer can help us connect with God and find peace in our lives. Prayer is a powerful tool that can help alleviate our worries and concerns. According to Matthew 6:25-34, we should turn to prayer when we feel anxious or fearful. Additionally, 1 Chronicles 16:11 reminds us to seek God's strength and guidance in all situations and to make prayer a constant part of our lives.

CONTROL YOUR THOUGHTS:
"Finally, brothers, whatever is true, whatever is noble, whatever is right, whatever is pure, whatever is lovely, whatever is admirable—if anything is excellent or praiseworthy—think about such things." (Philippians 4:8).
"We demolish arguments and every pretension that sets itself up against the knowledge of God, and we take captive every thought to make it obedient to Christ." (2 Corinthians 10:5).

When you are experiencing depression, it is important to take control of your thoughts and mental processes. This means actively monitoring and redirecting negative and self-defeating thoughts, as they can contribute to a downward spiral of emotions and exacerbate symptoms of depression. By consciously choosing to focus on positive thoughts and engaging in activities that bring you joy and fulfillment, you can help shift your mindset and improve your overall mental health. It may be challenging at first, but with practice and persistence, you can learn to manage your thoughts and emotions in a way that promotes well-being and resilience.

FOLLOW YOUR SPIRITUAL LEADERS.
"Whatever you have learned or received or heard from me, or seen in me—put it into practice. And the God of peace will be with you." (Philippians 4:9).
"Follow my example, as I follow the example of Christ." (1 Corinthians 11:1).
"Obey your leaders and submit to their authority. They keep watch over you as men who must give an account. Obey them so that their work will be a joy, not a burden, for that would be of no advantage to you." (Hebrews 13:17).

In moments of depression, it is advisable to seek guidance and support from your spiritual leaders. They can offer you the necessary guidance and direction to overcome your negative emotions and find solace in your faith. It is crucial to recognize that seeking spiritual counsel can help you reconnect with your inner self and find a sense of purpose in life. Your spiritual leaders can provide you with the tools and resources to deal with your negative emotions and help you navigate through the challenges you may be facing. Therefore, it is essential to stay connected with your spiritual community and seek their guidance and support during times of depression. Ultimately, following the advice of your spiritual leaders can help you find peace, hope, and healing during your darkest moments.

BE CONTENTED:
"I rejoice greatly in the Lord that at last you have renewed your concern for me. Indeed, you have been concerned, but you had no opportunity to show it. I am not saying this because I am in need, for I have learned to be content whatever the circumstances. I know what it is to be in need, and I know what it is to have plenty. I have learned the secret of being content in any and every situation, whether well fed or hungry, whether living in plenty or in want." (Philippians 4:10-12).

It is important to cultivate a sense of contentment to avoid falling into depression. This means finding satisfaction and happiness in the present moment, rather than constantly striving for more or feeling dissatisfied with what one has. By focusing on the positive aspects of one's life and practicing gratitude, one can cultivate a sense of contentment that can help protect against the negative effects of depression. Rather than constantly seeking external validation or comparing oneself to others, it is important to focus on one's own internal sense of well-being and happiness. This can involve engaging in activities that bring joy and fulfillment, developing positive relationships, and creating a sense of purpose and meaning in life. By prioritizing contentment and taking active steps to cultivate it, individuals can reduce their risk of developing depression and enjoy a more fulfilling and satisfying life.

BE POSITIVE:

"I can do everything through him who gives me strength." (Philippians 4:13).

To avoid depression, it is important to maintain a positive attitude. This means focusing on the good in life and approaching challenges with optimism and a mindset of growth. By cultivating a positive outlook, individuals can improve their mental health and overall well-being. It is also important to surround oneself with positive influences, such as supportive friends and family, and engage in activities that bring joy and fulfillment. Additionally, practicing self-care, such as exercise, healthy eating, and relaxation techniques, can also contribute to a more positive mindset. By prioritizing positivity in our thoughts and actions, we can protect ourselves from the harmful effects of depression and lead happier, healthier lives.

Chapter 7

Meditate Daily on These Bible Verses

Chapter 7
Meditate Daily on These Bible Verses

Isaiah 41:10
"Fear thou not; for I [am] with thee: be not dismayed; for I [am] thy God: I will strengthen thee; yea, I will help thee; yea, I will uphold thee with the right hand of my righteousness."

Philippians 4:6-8
"Be careful for nothing; but in everything by prayer and supplication with thanksgiving, let your requests be made known unto God."

Proverbs 3:5-6
"Trust in the LORD with all thine heart; and lean not unto thine own understanding."

1 Corinthians 10:13
"There hath no temptation taken you but such as is common to man: but God [is] faithful, who will not suffer you to be tempted above that ye are able; but will with the temptation also make a way to escape, that ye may be able to bear [it]."

1 Peter 5:7
"Casting all your care upon him; for the careth for you."

Proverbs 12:25
"Heaviness in the heart of man maketh it stoop: but a good word maketh it glad."

Matthew 6:34
"Take therefore no thought for the morrow: for the morrow shall take thought for the things of itself. Sufficient unto the day [is] the evil thereof."

James 5:15
"And the prayer of faith shall save the sick, and the Lord shall raise him up; and if he have committed sins, they shall be forgiven him."

Romans 8:26
"Likewise the Spirit also helpeth our infirmities: for we know not what we should pray for as we ought: but the Spirit itself maketh intercession for us with groanings which cannot be uttered."

Isaiah 41:13
"For I the LORD thy God will hold thy right hand, saying unto thee, Fear not; I will help thee."

Jeremiah 29:11
"For I know the thoughts that I think toward you, saith the LORD, thoughts of peace, and not of evil, to give you an expected end."

Romans 12:12
"Rejoicing in hope; patient in tribulation; continuing instant in prayer."

Hebrews 11:6
"But without faith [it is] impossible to please [him]: for he that cometh to God must believe that he is, and [that] he is a rewarder of them that diligently seek him."

Psalms 94:19
"In the multitude of my thoughts within me, thy comforts delight my soul."

Matthew 11:28-30
"Come unto me, all [ye] that labour and are heavy laden, and I will give you rest."

Romans 5:3-5
"And not only [so], but we glory in tribulations also: knowing that tribulation worketh patience."

Psalms 118:1-18
"O give thanks unto the LORD; for [he is] good: because his mercy [endureth] forever."

Psalms 34:17-18
"[The righteous] cry, and the LORD heareth, and delivereth them out of all their troubles."

Matthew 11:28
"Come unto me, all [ye] that labour and are heavy laden, and I will give you rest."

1 Peter 5:7
"Casting all your care upon him; for the careth for you."

Psalms 9:9
"The LORD also will be a refuge for the oppressed, a refuge in times of trouble."

2 Timothy 1:7
"For God hath not given us the spirit of fear; but of power, and of love, and of a sound mind."

Psalms 34:18
"The LORD [is] nigh unto them that are of a broken heart; and saveth such as be of a contrite spirit."

Revelation 21:4
"And God shall wipe away all tears from their eyes; and there shall be no more death, neither sorrow, nor crying, neither shall there be any more pain: for the former things are passed away."

John 10:10
"The thief cometh not, but for to steal, and to kill, and to destroy: I am come that they might have life, and that they might have [it] more abundantly."

John 16:33
"I have told you these things, so that in me you may have peace. In this world, you will have trouble. But take heart! I have overcome the world."

Isaiah 41:10
So do not fear, for I am with you; do not be dismayed, for I am your God. I will strengthen you and help you; I will uphold you with my righteous right hand."

Micah 7:7
"But me, I'm not giving up, I'm waiting for God to make things right."

1 Peter 5:10
"And after you've suffered a little while, the God of all grace will himself—restore, confirm, strengthen and establish you."

Ephesians 6:10
"Finally, be strong in The Lord and His almighty power."

Psalm 55:22
"Pile your troubles on God's shoulders—He will carry your load, He will help you out."

Psalm 27:1
"Light, space, zest—that's God! So, with God on my side, I'm afraid of no one and nothing."

Philippians 4:6-7

"Don't fret or worry, pray and the peace of God that transcends all understanding will guard your heart."

Romans 8:26-28

"The moment we get tired of waiting, God's spirit is alongside, helping us. It doesn't matter how we pray—God knows us; better than ourselves. God works all things for the good of those who love Him."

1 Peter 1:6

"So be truly glad there is wonderful joy ahead. Even though you have to endure many trials for a little while."

Isaiah 66:9

"I will not cause pain without allowing something new to be born, says The Lord."

Ecclesiastes 3:11

"He has made everything beautiful in its time."

Amen.

Chapter 8

Prayers to Kick Depression Out of Your Life

Chapter 8
Prayers to Kick Depression Out of Your Life

The biblical name for depression is Spirit of Heaviness. It is a dark shadow and burden which envelopes the soul of people and swallows their happiness.
Say, "To appoint unto them that mourn in Zion, to give unto them beauty for ashes, the oil of joy for mourning, the garment of praise for the spirit of heaviness; that they might be called trees of righteousness, the planting of the LORD, that he might be glorified." **Isaiah 61:3.**

● Power of a heavy heart, be dismantled, loose your hold upon my life in the name of Jesus.

● Holy Ghost fire, melt away every darkness of heaviness in my soul, in the name of Jesus.

● Let the garment of praise replace the spirit of heaviness in my life in Jesus' name.

● Power of God, move my life from strength to strength and from glory to glory in Jesus' name.

● I release myself from the power of discouragement in the name of Jesus.

● I reject every oppressive spirit hanging on my soul, in the name of Jesus.

● I come against the spirit of depression, despair, confusion, dejection, anxiety attack, fear, shame, spirit of guilt, spirit of frustration, and anything that has taken away my peace and tranquility, in the name of Jesus Christ.

● There shall be no more heaviness for my soul in Jesus name.

- I pull down every masked personality working against my happiness, in the name of Jesus.

- I dismantle every chain of darkness, arresting my freedom in the name of Jesus.

- Every thief that has been stealing from me, loose your power in the name of Jesus.

- I bury forever every yoke of heaviness, in the name of Jesus.

- I drink from the well of salvation in the name of Jesus.

- I refuse to be enslaved by the spirit of heaviness in the name of Jesus.

- Every power working against my mental health, be dismantled in the name of Jesus.

- Every burden of darkness enclosing my soul, clear away now, in the mighty name of Jesus

- I pray the Lord send the right people my way, that will offer me the help I need, in the mighty name of Jesus Christ.

About the Author

Joyce Oyelade is an incredible woman who wears many hats. Not only is she a devoted wife and mother, but she also has a deep passion for caring for others. With her extensive experience as a highly skilled nurse, Joyce has dedicated her life to the medical field, providing exceptional care and support to countless patients. In addition to her nursing degree, she has also pursued further education in the healthcare administration, allowing her to excel in leadership roles within the medical industry.

Joyce's diverse range of skills and experiences make her a force to be reckoned with. Her dedication to nursing, her unwavering faith, and her entrepreneurial spirit all contribute to her ability to make a lasting impact on the lives of others. But Joyce's talents don't stop there. She is a beacon of faith, serving as a minister of the gospel in the Oasis of Breakthrough International Church. Her strong spiritual beliefs guide her in all aspects of life, including her interactions with others and her unwavering commitment to helping those in need. Joyce is not only a nurturer of physical health but also a nurturer of souls. Her drive and determination led to her being appointed as the director of operations for Breakthrough International missions, where she plays a crucial role in coordinating and overseeing various initiatives aimed at bringing positive change to communities worldwide. Joyce Oyelade is happily married to Israel Oyelade.

References:

Mayo Foundation for Medical Education and Research. (n.d.). *Depression.* Mayo Clinic.

Raypole, C. (2021, May 24). *Spiritual depression: Signs, causes, coping, and treatment*

Cover Design and Page Layout
@Say It Loud Africa IG@Sayitloudafrica +234 703 88 51 322

Made in the USA
Middletown, DE
25 October 2023

41283291R00027